HowExper
Door to Door Sales

101 Tips to Learn How to Sell Door to Door and Become an Excellent Door to Door Salesman

HowExpert with Brandon Crawford

For more tips related to this topic, visit HowExpert.com/doortodoorsales.

Recommended Resources

- HowExpert.com – Quick 'How To' Guides on All Topics from A to Z by Everyday Experts.
- HowExpert.com/free – Free HowExpert Email Newsletter.
- HowExpert.com/books – HowExpert Books
- HowExpert.com/courses – HowExpert Courses
- HowExpert.com/clothing – HowExpert Clothing
- HowExpert.com/membership – HowExpert Membership Site
- HowExpert.com/affiliates – HowExpert Affiliate Program
- HowExpert.com/jobs – HowExpert Jobs
- HowExpert.com/writers – Write About Your #1 Passion/Knowledge/Expertise & Become a HowExpert Author.
- HowExpert.com/resources – Additional HowExpert Recommended Resources
- YouTube.com/HowExpert – Subscribe to HowExpert YouTube.
- Instagram.com/HowExpert – Follow HowExpert on Instagram.
- Facebook.com/HowExpert – Follow HowExpert on Facebook.
- TikTok.com/@HowExpert – Follow HowExpert on TikTok.

Publisher's Foreword

Dear HowExpert Reader,

HowExpert publishes quick 'how to' guides on all topics from A to Z by everyday experts.

At HowExpert, our mission is to discover, empower, and maximize everyday people's talents to ultimately make a positive impact in the world for all topics from A to Z...one everyday expert at a time!

All of our HowExpert guides are written by everyday people just like you and me, who have a passion, knowledge, and expertise for a specific topic.

We take great pride in selecting everyday experts who have a passion, real-life experience in a topic, and excellent writing skills to teach you about the topic you are also passionate about and eager to learn.

We hope you get a lot of value from our HowExpert guides, and it can make a positive impact on your life in some way. All of our readers, including you, help us continue living our mission of positively impacting the world for all spheres of influences from A to Z.

If you enjoyed one of our HowExpert guides, then please take a moment to send us your feedback from wherever you got this book.

Thank you, and we wish you all the best in all aspects of life.

Sincerely,

BJ Min
Founder & Publisher of HowExpert
HowExpert.com

PS...If you are also interested in becoming a HowExpert author, then please visit our website at HowExpert.com/writers. Thank you & again, all the best!

Table of Contents

Chapter 1: A Brief History and Summary of Door-to-Door Sales

Door-to-door sales is a direct-to-consumer style of selling that has been utilized for nearly 150 years. Sales reps interact face-to-face with possible customers, prospecting residential areas on foot by knocking on doors. Attempting to engage homeowners in a potential conversation regarding their products or services, door-to-door salespeople rely heavily on a structured set of steps that outline a successful sale.

The job of a door-to-door salesman has an incredibly high turnover rate because the wages usually are entirely commission-based. For the average member of the workforce, this can be extremely intimidating. On the other hand, being in control of how much money I earned was a benefit for me. In addition, I considered myself a people person and had a knack for persuading people.

When I first started selling door-to-door, the lengthy history and statistics were sold to me daily. The door-to-door sales industry is one of the oldest surviving means of earning a living in America. In the late 1700s and early 1800s, traveling salesman navigated growing cities and towns via horse-drawn covered wagons that housed their wares. In demand, supplies such as medicine and other goods were commonly peddled door-to-door.

In 1886 the Avon company first opened its doors for business. David H. McConnell was a seasoned traveling book salesman. During his time selling books, David noticed that women were far more interested in items like perfume and other cosmetics that were offered as samples in his books. The rest is history.

The industry witnessed an explosion in the 1950s and 1960s. Employed as a clever marketing tactic, sales companies saw an ideal customer in housewives and stay-at-home moms. So while dad was at work, door-to-door salesmen pitched cosmetics, encyclopedias, vacuum cleaners, and kitchen appliances to nearly every housewife in America.

Since that time, almost every product you could imagine has been sold door-to-door. Everyday products and services included frozen foods, appliances, magazines, cleaning products, toys, pest-control jobs, cable and internet services, solar panels, and roofing. In 2021 the industry persists.

In an industry that has survived nearly two centuries, I felt a sense of confidence and security where others feared instability and inconsistency. This view on things is the prime reason why I was so successful at selling door-to-door.

Why Are Door-to-Door Sales Still Effective?

In an era where e-commerce and digital marketing dominate a good portion of the market, door-to-door sales continue to thrive. There are several reasons why door-to-door sales are still profitable.

Word of Mouth Advertising

The sales rep who trained me relayed a vital piece of information that I will never forget. Word of mouth is the best form of advertising. Companies pay billions of dollars for advertisements every year. Yet, it costs next to nothing to send a sales rep door-to-door as an ambassador for your brand.

Tip #1. Using word of mouth is one of the best ways to advertise your product and entice new clients. When you make a sale, ask the customer for three to five referrals they can send you to. Make a list of these referrals and see them immediately after the current sale. Be sure to use the existing customer's name when you contact these referrals.

Consumers are bombarded with advertising campaigns from every platform imaginable. It is true; there is a high level of success due to these campaigns. However, there is no replacing human-to-human interaction. Dealing with someone face-to-face extracts high levels of emotion, leading to triggers that lead to a sale. Greater levels of attention and care are put into a door-to-door sale.

The best way to measure the success of a direct sale is by comparing the conversion rates between a door-to-door sale and an online ad campaign. A good online ad campaign will convert at a level of around 10%, which is considered outstanding in the digital market. A good door-to-door salesperson, however, will have a conversion rate between 40 and 60 percent.

Tip #2. A good salesperson will always keep a score sheet. First, use a journal to track the number of doors you knock on and how many times you contact a live person. Next, keep track of the number of people you demo your product for in a separate column. Finally, keep a count of how many of the demos end up becoming a closed sale. It allows you to track your success percentages and closing rates.

Less Competition

In prior decades door-to-door sales were the most common way of purchasing any goods or services. Those days are long gone. The e-commerce and internet marketing worlds are incredibly competitive. Advertisers constantly compete to outbid and outperform each other.

The digital market is the new gold rush, and everyone wants to make money online. As a result, door-to-door sales have seen a decrease in registered and licensed agents, which means less competition. In addition, the industry witnessed a "cooling down" period in the early 2000s as stricter laws forced businesses operating illegally to shut their doors. It left only professional and customer-service-driven companies to take over the market.

Tip #3. Look for areas with smaller numbers of registered door-to-door sales companies. These areas are less likely to be used to having someone knocking on their door to sell them a product. Typically, this means they'll be more interested and eager to speak with you about what you have for sale.

The last few years have seen a steady increase in sales for the door-to-door companies that remain open. Although the industry has been on the decline, the success rates per company have been growing.

Easy to Adapt

Digital marketing, product research, graphic design, and public relations are all key elements in e-commerce. Extensive amounts of time and money are put into product launching. Nearly every vital role involved in an online business is outsourced. It can become incredibly expensive. One failed product can spell disaster.

There are fewer operating costs involved in door-to-door sales. Companies can also easily adapt and make changes that are needed to fine-tune their conversion rates. An outside sales team acts as product research staff, ambassador, and product launcher. Going directly to the consumer with the product handles all the vital elements of marketing simultaneously.

Easier to Measure Profits and Success

There are so many factors that contribute to the success of a digital sales campaign. Hundreds of different dynamics can sway a sale one way or another, and consumers have millions of options at their fingertips. As a result, it can be challenging to measure what works and what does not.

In the world of door-to-door sales, three major elements make or break a deal - it's either you, the product, or the money. All objections can be handled by addressing one of those three factors. There is no question whether a door-to-door campaign has reached the desired levels of success.

Tip #4. It's either you, the product, or the money. So, first, use this tip to analyze all sales when the consumer objects to buying. Then, get used to handling these objections when they're brought up by practicing rebuttals for each of them, respectively.

People Love Buying from People

A digital ad cannot make eye contact or address the immediate needs of an individual. Data can do its best to qualify a target audience, but the experience does not translate the same.

A good door-to-door salesman will build a good rapport with a potential customer. He will connect with them emotionally, ask the right questions, and address their needs. But, more importantly, a good salesperson can show concern. The bottom line is a much higher level of trust is established during a door-to-door sale. If someone trusts you enough to let you in their home, most likely they trust you enough to buy from you.

Tip #5. Get personal with your customer and build trust. For example, look them in the eye, use their first name when speaking to them, and give them a firm handshake. These actions can make a customer feel more comfortable.

Are Door-to-Door Salesmen Successful?

Usually, after telling someone that I was a door-to-door salesman, I always seemed to receive the same follow-up question from everyone. "Are you successful? Do you make any money doing that?" is something I got used to hearing constantly. But, of course, the simple answer to that question is absolutely. My door-to-door sales career was incredibly successful, and many door-to-door salespeople live extremely comfortable lives.

The job of a door-to-door salesman can be challenging, but it is also gratifying. Success levels of a door-to-door sales rep are based on a variety of factors. Therefore, any potential door-to-door sales rep should carefully examine these key elements whenever beginning a career with a company.

Commission Structure

What type of commission exists, and what is the paygrade? Commission-only jobs typically have a set price a salesman pays for the product or service they are selling. Any successful sale that is made for a dollar amount higher than the cost of the product means the salesman can keep the difference. This type of commission structure is better suited for an experienced salesperson with a high close ratio, and salesmen that get paid this way fall under independent contractor status. My first sales job consisted of this type of commission. Not having a base pay sharpened me as a salesman and made me hungrier.

Gross margin means the salesman will receive a gross percentage of the total sale. For example, if a deal is made for $2,000, and the cost associated with the sale is $1,000, the salesman will profit $1,000. Thus, sales reps earn the most on sales with higher margins. Conversely, on sales with extremely low margins, the payout may be considerably lower than anticipated.

Tiered commission or a sliding scale means different pay percentages are earned based on varying levels of total sales. For example, a salesperson may make 15% on anything up to $10,000. Anything above $10,000 leads to a bonus of 10%, meaning the total commission is 25%. There are varying degrees and percentages with this style of commission, which pushes salesman to continue to sell beyond their quota in the hopes of earning bonus money.

Tip #6. Always be sure to get your commission structure in writing. Ensure all the details are clear between you and the manager and any bonus structures that might be included on a daily and weekly basis.

Product Quality/Brand Reputation

The quality of the products and services a salesman has access to are extremely important. This factor weighs heavily on the success of a door-to-door salesman, especially if they sell at a state or regional level and depend on repeat business. A satisfied customer is a repeat customer.

A good brand or company reputation can go a long way in the sales industry. Checking for online reviews of the company can tell you a lot about how they operate. For example, do they handle their customer service calls well? Do they honor the three-day buyer's right to cancel? Are customers generally happy with the tactics of the salesman and products they purchased?

Tip #7. Don't be afraid to use the internet to your advantage when you have a good product. Ask your customers to leave you a favorable review regarding the product and your behavior as a salesman. A good review goes a long way when it comes to new customers.

It is vital to be sure that the company holds a standard for ethical sales practices. A good door-to-door sales company will never train their salesman to lie about the product. It is not necessary to make up an outrageous story about why you are at someone's door. Keeping it simple and being honest is the most effective method. People can sense when something is not right or they are being lied to. Honesty is the best policy in any sales environment.

Work Environment

Is the atmosphere of the company professional and generally positive? These two factors are extremely crucial to a door-to-door salesman's success. Habits and attitudes spread like wildfire. Therefore, surrounding yourself with professional and positive people can positively impact your state of mind.

Some of the best advice I ever received as a door-to-door salesman was being advised to treat it like a career. Do not become too relaxed or lazy when it comes to your approach. Be on time, remain professional, treat your customers with respect, and keep all your business clean. Do not cut corners or try to do things the easy way.

The prospect of fast cash and big commissions can lead a salesman to become complacent or develop "big paycheck syndrome." However, when you land a big sale, it is not time to take a week off. That's when you push even harder.

**Tip #8. Not giving up or settling is key in the sales industry. When you're hot, push harder. It leads to more success as opposed to remaining complacent.**

Keeping a sales office competitive is extremely important and can drive sales through the roof. I remember when the company I worked for ran quota and production contests, it used to motivate me to perform higher. I wanted to win every competition and be at the top of the board every week. A good sales office will make the numbers a priority. Chase the numbers, and the money will become a byproduct.

Is There Room for Advancement?

Talented sales reps can eventually make good managers or crew leaders. A good door-to-door sales company will have multiple options for advancement. Nobody wants to knock on doors forever, and higher positions can lead to passive income from the reps who knock door-to-door.

Higher positions typically include crew leader, territory manager, corporate trainer, assistant manager, office manager, sales manager, regional manager, and national manager. After six months of selling door-to-door, I was rewarded with the general manager position at the office I worked at. However, I remained competitive in the field after becoming a manager. A manager who remains in the field will command more respect from his sales reps.

The potential for advancement will produce company loyalty. Sales reps have a higher chance of sticking around if they know there is some longevity and room for growth. In addition, many door-to-door sales companies offer a stake as an owner, allowing a sales rep to open their own location and stock in the company.

Tip #9. If you have friends who need work, encourage them to try a position at the door-to-door company you work for. Many door-to-door companies will pay bonuses or a percentage if you bring in new door knockers.

Chapter 1 Review

1. Door-to-door sales have been successful for nearly two centuries and are still a practical way to earn a living.

2. Nearly any product imaginable can and has been sold door-to-door.
3. Low operating costs, direct human contact, and lower competition levels have attributed to the continued success of door-to-door sales.
4. Commission structure, work environment, and product quality are the most critical factors in a door-to-door sales office.
5. Longevity and job security are very realistic in door-to-door sales by focusing on company advancement. As a result, management positions and ownership opportunities exist at nearly every door-to-door sales company.

Chapter 2: Different Types of Door-to-Door Sales

In the world of door-to-door sales, there is salesman known as "outside sales reps," and there are "inside sales reps." Outside sales reps can hunt for deals anywhere they wish. These sales can be obtained through parking lots, businesses, residential areas, or any retail location. In addition, they can contact any human being they come across.

Tip #10. If you want better odds and a chance to gain more experience, consider becoming an outside sales rep. Your target demographic has a much broader range, and the amount of people you can contact is substantially higher.

Inside sales reps usually must stick to premade appointments strictly in residential areas. However, some companies will allow their sales reps to cold-knock doors between these premade appointments to canvass for new leads and sales.

Door-to-door sales companies all rely on door-knocking and contacting homeowners to generate sales. These contacts can either be made by cold-calling or through pre-scheduled appointments.

Tip #11. Usually, these pre-scheduled appointments are set up by lower-level door knockers who canvas a neighborhood for leads. If you begin in one of these positions, understand you won't receive a commission unless the salesman you set up the appointment for closes the sale

There are two categories that a door-to-door sales company can potentially be grouped into based on the way they provide their products or services. Only two methods exist for a product or service to be delivered when a sale is made from a door-to-door sale.

The company either has the product already on hand, in which case their salesman is considered peddlers. However, if the product is unavailable immediately and must be delivered or installed at a later agreed-upon date, the salesman would be viewed as a solicitor.

Peddlers have their wares available on hand, while solicitors make their goods or services available later, sometime after the initial sale. Generally, both types of door-to-door salesman will require special permits when conducting business within a town or city limits.

Tip #12. Peddlers tend to receive higher commissions for several reasons. First, when the sales rep can carry their product with them, building value is easier by showing the customer an example. Second, it's easier to ask for larger amounts of money on high-ticket items because more value is built. Solicitors usually offer lower-priced items, leading to lower commissions.

There are only a few instances when a door-to-door salesperson will not need a permit or license to conduct business.

- If they are selling a farm or garden product, they produce themselves
- Are representing a non-commercial educational organization
- If they are a food vendor already licensed through the appropriate authorities
- Are a part of a city-sponsored event

There are hundreds, if not thousands, of different door-to-door sales companies with tens of thousands of products and services at the helm. So let's examine the two distinct company categories and the elements that make them unique from one another.

Selling Services Delivered Later (Solicitor)

A door-to-door salesman who sells a product or service delivered or made available later is known as a solicitor. Typically, this type of door-to-door salesman carries a list or catalog of some sort with the products or services his company has available.

There might be a demo product of each different type of item he has for sale for the sake of showing the customer an example of the product. Usually, once this type of sale is finalized, the salesman produces a pre-written contract that the customer can examine.

The contract is signed with a final price point. Usually, an agreed-upon date is included in the contract that contains information about when the goods or services will be delivered.

Sometimes these types of sales will also be broken down into different installments or payments. This information will also be included in the signed contract.

Tip #13. Explain the importance of making their payments on time. The remainder of your commission on this sale is contingent on them following through with their payment obligations. Never discuss this information with a customer; instead, convey the message in a way that highlights the importance of the payment because of the credit ramifications.

Salesman Compensation

Usually, the payment for this type of sale will be broken down between front-end and back-end commission payments for the salesman. If there is a down payment, the salesman will receive a portion of this on the front-end.

Depending on the structure of the payment plan and when the goods or services are delivered, the salesman will receive the rest of their commission once the contract is fulfilled. If the contract or payments are broken and altered in any way, this could affect the final commission for the salesman.

Common Types of Door-to-Door Solicitation Companies

There are thousands of different door-to-door companies that rely on cold solicitations to generate revenue for the company. These are the most common types of companies and industries seen using this method of sales generation.

Tip #14. Specific industries will experience surges in sales and popularity based on a variety of factors. Stay updated on trends and sales patterns to stick with an industry that's producing sales at a high volume.

1. Door-to-door Cable/Internet Sales

Door-to-door cable and internet salespeople are seen canvassing neighborhoods and developments throughout the country all year. Their sales aren't seasonal and remain steady throughout the year.

These salesmen will typically wear company badges to represent themselves and a shirt with the company logo. The salesman will either work for a company contracted by the cable or internet company to generate new sales or directly for the cable or internet company.

Usually, these reps will offer the customer a deal to switch their cable package or upgrade to a better bundle. Many times, the salesmen will receive bonuses if the customer changes from a different company.

The commission on these sales is generally based on a customer signing some form of a 12-month contract. The customer signs a contract for a period and agrees to have the service installed within a reasonable amount of time. The situation is then passed off to the telecommunications company who is now under contract with the customer.

2. *Door-to-Door Energy Deregulation*

Door-to-door energy deregulation has become increasingly popular in the last few years. In the past, giant companies held monopolies over the energy sector, leaving customers with few options for sourcing their electricity and gas.

Deregulation laws changed this as one-by-one states chose to open the market to smaller companies. It led to an explosion of door-to-door sales companies offering the energy services provided by these new, smaller companies.

The contract with these companies works like any other solicitation. First, there is a period where a customer will be placed under contract. Then, there is usually an agreed-upon amount of savings worked into the deal that entices the customer to make the switch, to begin with.

The salesman will be paid either all the commission upfront or in installments based on customer payments. As a result, energy deregulation sales typically aren't canceled because customers have substantial savings compared to doing business with their previous energy supplier.

Tip #15. New industries like deregulation are always lucrative. Solar is another similar industry that's considered a hot commodity. Both of these sectors are gaining popularity among homeowners, and you can use that in your sales pitch. Any product that saves a homeowner a large amount of money is an easy sale, and deregulation does just that.

3. Door-to-Door Pest Control Sales

Door-to-door pest control salespeople scout neighborhoods, looking for customers who want to purchase new or upgraded extermination services. This type of sales job is usually seasonal, as most pests begin to die out in the fall and winter.

Normally a pest control salesman receives a list of prior customers that subscribed to extermination services. They will target these customers first, then move on to general cold knocking.

If a customer is interested, the salesman will perform a routine inspection of the home and surrounding property. This inspection will allow the salesman to compile a list of services that may suit the homeowner best.

The inspection may include an assessment of the types of bugs and nests that have been located and other trouble areas, including sitting water. Generally, the customer will be offered some form of organic alternative as well.

4. Door-to-Door Roofing Sales

Door-to-door roofing salesmen are also known as storm chasers. It is because the companies they work for purposely locate areas that have been impacted by severe storms or hurricanes.

Many homes have damaged roofs in these areas, and several companies will converge on hard-hit areas often days before the storm even hits. This industry is highly competitive because of the high commissions.

Usually, a roofing company will use drone flyovers to locate homes with the most damage and send the salesman directly to those homes. Once the customer agrees, the salesman will scale a ladder to inspect the severity of the destruction.

After this period, the insurance company is contacted to ensure the customer the repairs will be covered by their insurance. Once this confirmation is complete, the insurance company sends an adjuster out to survey the damage.

The salesperson will usually receive a small percentage upfront once the deductible is paid and the job is under contract. After the insurance company pays the roofers for the completed job, the salesman will receive the remainder of the commission.

Tip #16. Door-to-door roofing repair companies boast some of the highest commissions in the industry. It's not uncommon for top-level sales reps in this industry to earn close to seven figures per year.

5. Door-to-Door Magazine Sales

Door-to-door magazine companies are still in existence but are quickly fading. The internet has taken its toll on this industry in more ways than one.

Few people are subscribing to magazines, and the industry has also received many unfavorable reviews and writeups in the last decade. However, there are a few survivors who conduct business the right way.

A salesman canvasses neighborhoods and apartments, offering magazine subscription sales. These are sold in 12-, 24-, and 48-months increments. The entire duration must be paid in full before the transaction is finalized.

Once the sale clears with the publishing company, the salesman will receive their commission. It's long been stated in the sales industry that this type of door-to-door sales breeds some of the strongest producers in the door-to-door sector.

Selling Services Available Immediately (Peddler)

When door-to-door salespeople have their wares and items available for immediate receival, they are considered peddlers. A peddler exchanges the money for services or goods that the customer receives at the time of sale.

Salesman Compensation

Usually, with this type of door-to-door sale, a peddler will receive his commission for the entire sale the same week the sale is completed. There is no contract involved, and the goods are usually paid for in full by the end of the transaction, so there's no need for a structured commission payout.

The only exception to this is if a customer purchases an item on a payment plan or credit. In this case, there may be a structured commission payout based on the payoff of the product or services.

Common Types of Door-to-Door Peddlers

These are some of the most popular types of door-to-door companies that peddle.

1. Door-to-Door Meat Sales

This was the industry I broke into when beginning my door-to-door sales career. Believe me; it was lucrative.

All salesman received a company vehicle, usually a Toyota Tacoma pickup truck with a refrigeration unit on the back. The unit was loaded with various steak, chicken, seafood, and pork products.

Everybody was equipped with a menu with the prices of these various packages. Then, we would hit the road to canvass neighborhoods, businesses, and country roads starting in the morning. Sometimes our days wouldn't end until 8 or 9 at night.

Customers could pay with cash, check, or credit card. After knocking on the door and getting the hook, we would show the customer the different wholesale meat options we had on the truck. Once they agreed, we'd pack the items in their freezer for them.

Personally, my biggest sale ever was for $18,546. My commission on that sale was over $8,000. Of course, I was paid out my commission that same night.

During my peak, I earned over $3,000 per week consistently as a door-to-door steak salesman. The money was consistent, and the lessons I learned were priceless.

Obtaining repeat customers was a regular thing, and I'd return to sell them more as often as I could. Sometimes I'd even sell them a brand-new freezer I threw in on the deal.

Tip #17. If you want an industry that's evergreen and recession-proof, you can't go wrong with selling food door-to-door. Everybody eats, and it's an expense that can't be avoided. For example, during the 2008 recession when other sales industries were tanking, I had no problem clearing six figures that year in my first-year full year as a sales rep.

2. Door-to-Door Vacuum Sales

When people think of door-to-door sales, a vacuum salesman is a picture they get in their heads. For some reason, vacuum salespeople are synonymous with the term door-to-door salesman. I guess it's because, as kids, most everyone went through the experience of a carpet demo or their parents negotiating with a vacuum salesperson.

These salesmen usually travel in groups of two or three in a car or van. They carry an assortment of vacuums or floor cleaners in the vehicle with them, ready to find a new home for these items in the form of a homeowner.

After the customer is hooked, the salesman will retrieve a demo vacuum from the vehicle. Sometimes these demos can take hours to complete. After all the vacuum features are displayed, the customer is offered the vacuum for an agreed-upon lump sum, or a payment plan is set up.

If a payment plan is set up, the salesman will not receive the entire commission on that week's check. Instead, based on the plan, their commission will be divided into payments and completed once the customer's payment obligations are finalized.

3. *Door-to-Door Tool Salesman*

Typically, these salesmen prefer to canvass cities and towns looking for construction sites or new housing developments still under construction. Scouring parking lots is also a prevalent method of finding new customers.

These sales reps will travel with a pickup truck full of tools. Usually, this will be a full pallet's worth of tools. These toolsets will consist of nearly every device you could think of—socket sets, screwdriver sets, impact wrenches, drills, saws of various types, and generators.

Basically, these are kits you could use to construct a whole house. The reps carry price sheets with them that display a retail price for each tool individually and the package.

The salesman pitch various reasons as to why they have the tools to offer for sale. Sometimes these salesmen are a part of larger construction companies or wholesale outlets who get them for discounted prices.

After showing the potential buyer the retail prices, they attempt to sell the whole set as a bundle at wholesale. If the customer doesn't bite on the package, the salesman will continue to sell the set pieces for a discount.

Tip #18. This tip goes for tools and electronics sales; the customer will probably ask for some type of demo. It's vital that you work for a reputable company that provides you with proper equipment for sale so you can navigate these situations. Otherwise, they're just setting you up for failure.

4. Door-to-Door Electronics Salesman

This door-to-door sector died off for a bit but has recently seen new life. In the middle the to late 1990s, white vans were seen in droves scouring mall parking lots and other retail spaces attempting to sell discounted home and audio speakers.

These speakers were typically low quality and not the top-brand caliber salesman promised. It led to a negative reputation for a lot of these companies.

However, in the late 2010s, a rise in wholesale electronic availability and a newfound homeowner interest in home theater brought this industry back to life. As a result, more credible electronics companies have begun popping up, choosing to knock on doors rather than peddle in parking lots.

These more reputable companies offer warranties on their products and higher-quality options. Some of them even offer free installation after the items are purchased.

The sales process and demo work just like the tool industry. The salesman will have a more extensive set of electronics equipment they are looking to market and sell at wholesale prices instead of the retail figures listed on their brochure or price sheet.

5. *Door-to-Door Chemical Cleaner Salesman*

The door-to-door chemical cleaner company is another sales industry known to produce extraordinarily strong salesman. These reps will enter neighborhoods to sell homeowners various window, floor, and concrete cleaning products.

Usually, the rep will knock on the door and hopefully get invited into the home. The agent will ask the homeowner what their biggest trouble spot is regarding cleanliness.

Sales reps will have the homeowner retrieve the regular cleaner they would purchase at the grocery store. Then, doing a side-by-side demo, the agent will show the homeowner the superior quality of the cleaning products they have on hand.

Once the homeowner is convinced, the sales reps offer the homeowners bottles of the cleaner in bulk discounts. The more they buy, the better the deal. The cleaners are marketed as highly potent and can typically be diluted.

Tip #19. Selling lower-priced items like cleaners bring lower commissions. However, you can remedy this and still make a great living by pushing volume. Offer savings on purchases of multiple units, and don't be afraid to upsell.

Most of the cleaners come with some form of guarantee and the ability to reorder after their original supply has been used. The total price must be paid at the time of sale, so there's no waiting on a structured commission payout.

Chapter 2 Review

1. The two types of door-to-door salesman are peddlers and solicitors.
2. Peddlers have their goods on hand, while solicitors make their goods or services available later.
3. Peddlers typically get paid their commission faster than solicitors.
4. Solicitors typically offer payment plans as part of their payment options.
5. Services are generally sold more under the guise of a solicitation, while peddlers generally sell items.

Chapter 3: Preparing to Sell Door-to-Door

When it comes to the profession of door-to-sales rep, several key elements factor into obtaining success. Formulating an effective strategy and setting goals based on specific periods can help you manifest a favorable outcome.

Tip #20. Always be sure to set goals based on time. For example, have a one-week goal, a two-week goal, a monthly goal, a six-month goal, a yearly goal, etc. It helps you maintain accountability for yourself.

Maintaining a successful career in door-to-door sales takes discipline and focus. Entering the world of commission-based sales can be a challenging transition to make when an individual is used to an hourly paycheck or uniform salary.

Besides changes to the method of payment, the work atmosphere and culture are also noticeably different. For example, door-to-door sales require a certain level of independence and self-motivation that generally isn't needed for a nine-to-five position.

Tip #21. It's crucial that you manage your independence responsibly. Commission salespeople need to be highly self-motivated and able to challenge themselves daily.

When I initially began my journey into the door-to-door workforce, every aspect was utterly foreign to me. The most appealing part was the potential to earn wages that I had never seen from an hourly position. I was young, in a new part of the country, and I was hungry. Placed in any other setting, I'm fairly confident that I would have achieved success. However, because of my newfound situation and an unquenchable thirst for the almighty dollar, my motivation spread through me like wildfire when I saw the earning potential.

It takes an attitude like this to exist at the top rung of door-to-door sales. An unmatched level of energy combined with financial discipline and strict dedication to your goals can make a sales rep unstoppable. Despite my initial excitement, in the beginning, I had no idea the type of success that was in store for me in the coming months. But that's the level my mind was operating on.

Tip #22. The best salesman has exceptionally high energy levels. It's important to keep this energy at all times in the office and in the field as it translates to coworkers and customers.

I didn't realize it at the time, but selling door-to-door helped mold me into an incredibly strong sales rep. If I knew back then what I know now, I would've kept a few crucial points in mind while acclimating to the business.

To be honest, while I did enjoy success fairly quickly, there was about a three-week period where I crashed and burned. In my first week, I jumpstarted right to success, made some money, and then hit a wall. I guess you could attribute that first week to pure energy.

That energy is what propelled me to a high point after my first week. Unfortunately, entering my second week, I had two bad days to start the week. That energy and positivity that powered me through my first week quickly turned to anxiety and discouragement.

Unable to pull myself out of this funk and with no prior knowledge of how to deal with buyers, I sunk like a stone. For the next three weeks, I barely made money, and I almost quit the business.

Luckily, a sales rep from one of the other locations was dispatched to come to retrain me. I guess the manager saw my potential and wanted to do everything he could to stop me from quitting.

I was fortunate that the rep who took me under his wing was a diamond in the rough. He's one of the best salesmen I've ever met, and I stay in touch with him to this day. His charisma was off the charts, and his attitude was contagious. But most importantly, he knew the science of sales.

Tip #23. If you hit a slump or a dry patch with very little commission, look to the top producers for advice. Ask one of them to take you under their wing or provide you with some of their best tips. Shadow them and listen to how they speak, and watch how they move; these are essential mannerisms to learn.

He taught me several tips and tricks that I should have been taught from the beginning but wasn't. These were fundamentals of the door-to-door business that any new rep should learn before knocking on their first door. What he taught me is what I'm sharing with you in this section.

Important Points to Remember

In my opinion, these are the most important points that any new sales rep should carry with them going into their first day on the job. They help you understand certain elements of sales when you hit bumps or start to become negative. Also, whenever you hit a point of frustration (which you will), normally, one or all of these points can help you power through those emotions.

Get Used to Hearing "No"

In door-to-door sales, you will be told no; and it will happen a lot. One of the first things the rep who retrained me said after we got in the truck was, "you know they're going to tell us no today, right?" I didn't quite understand the power of the tip he was giving me.

Tip #24. Get used to hearing the word no throughout your day. You will listen to the word no more than you will listen to yes.

He said it sarcastically, almost to highlight the fact that it was comical we would hear the word no, and it didn't bother him. I felt like there was something he knew that I didn't; this ended up being more accurate than I could have imagined.

In my career as a door knocker, I've had a weapon pulled on me, I've been called the worst names in the book, I've had the police called on me, and I've had an owner unleash their dog on me. Believe it or not, I've had all of these incidents happen in one day.

Tip #25. Be prepared for any negative situation that might come your way. Don't let these events get to you or ruin your attitude. Shrug it off, and keep moving.

For the average person, one of these incidents would be enough to send them packing without looking back. But, thankfully, I'm not the average person, and you must look at yourself the same.

Remember that your rate of success when it comes to knocking on doors will be about ten to twenty percent. What do I mean by this?

If you knock on ten doors, one or two of those doors will allow you to take the sale to the next step and perform a demo. In the industry

I was in, this meant showing them packages of frozen steak and seafood.

Tip #26. If you're managing to get ten to twenty percent of the doors you knock on interested in the product, you're doing fine. Twenty percent of the houses participating in a demo will lead to your quota and standard success rates.

Your close rate, which is the percentage of people you make a sale to after showing them a demo, should be much higher than ten or twenty percent, but we will cover that later. Just understand this one crucial point for now; if you factor in sales you make in places other than residential neighborhoods (gas stations, parking lots, etc.), seventy percent of the people you encounter are going to tell you no.

Tip #27. Around seventy percent of the people you encounter will end up telling you no. It's nothing you're doing wrong; it's just the law of averages. Sales is a numbers game.

I didn't understand this when I hit my slump. My first week in the business, I was running on pure adrenaline and excitement, and I didn't even think about the people who told me no when I pitched to them. The fact that I was closing deals was enough to take the sting away from any rejection I encountered.

Unaware that being told no was a normal part of the business, when I became aware of the rejection, I was snapped back to reality. It made me feel like there was something I was doing wrong.

In reality, there were things that I was doing wrong that needed some work, but my performance wasn't subpar to the point of having a zero percent close rate, and that's precisely what I had when I hit my slump.

My attitude is what held me back. I wasn't prepared for the fact that dealing with being told no so often was an everyday occurrence, and it made my sales pitch sound desperate and forced. It is a deal killer 99.9% of the time. Customers will sense how you feel, and the balance of your attitude and usually will match this energy in an exchange called "mirroring."

Tip #28. Most of the time, a bad attitude is what causes door-to-door salesman to fail. Unfortunately, this negativity can be sensed by customers, and usually, it rubs off on them.

Another point that I wasn't aware of also has to do with being told no. The ultimate goal is to find a yes; this is what leads to the money. However, did you know that sometimes it's more beneficial to quickly arrive at a no instead of digging for a yes?

Find the "No's" Faster

Despite running into the occasional rude homeowner, most of the people I encountered knocking on doors were surprisingly pleasant. I'd say eighty percent of the people I contacted throughout the day were cordial. Of those eighty percent, I'd say that fifty percent of them were willing to engage in a conversation with me, with the other twenty percent directly welcoming me into their homes.

Ideally, you want to be invited into the home of a customer to close the deal. They're more comfortable in their home, and it's just a more personal situation overall. If someone invites you into their home, most likely they trust you. But we'll go into greater detail on this topic later.

Tip #29. When you're about to do a demo, you always want to get invited into the home. If a customer trusts you enough to invite you into their home, most likely they trust you enough to buy from you.

The problem with some of the people that engaged with me and allowed me into their homes was that they had no interest in buying from the start. Many people are too nice, sometimes lacking the ability to say no from the start.

It may seem polite and better than receiving a hard no; however, this couldn't be further from the truth. When I was in the prime of my career, I found myself looking for no's faster. These people that are overly polite end up killing valuable time you have in the field. It is time spent on a situation with no chance of a sale when you could otherwise find homeowners better suited for your product.

One of the best pieces of advice I ever received in the business was directly related to this topic. "Every no gets you closer to a yes." It is one of the truest statements associated with the door-to-door sales business. In door-to-door sales, we play the numbers game, working the odds as the day progresses.

It doesn't happen in any set order because your money doesn't care what time of day you make it. The first half of the day, you might encounter fifty prospects that tell you no over and over again. Eventually, you'll hit a patch where you get five yeses back-to-back. Or, your day may be evenly distributed with some yes's here, some no's there, and sales in between. These are how most days will look if you're a consistent sales rep.

Tip #30. Every no brings you closer to a yes. The faster you get the no's out of the way, the quicker you get to a sale.

Many sales reps lived for days where they hit three or four doors and sold out before noon. Don't get me wrong; those days are sweet. However, the competitor in me found a sense of gratification after getting beat down all day with no's and finally digging deep to claim victory during the last hour of business. I compare this to hitting a game-winning shot in the final seconds of basketball. There's no feeling in the world quite like this.

As you progress in your career as a sales rep, you'll learn to distinguish between a hard no, a soft no, and people that are just yanking your chain. In the beginning, you'll grind every customer in the hopes of turning every no into a yes. When you gain experience, becoming more seasoned, you'll know when to walk away to save those valuable seconds and minutes. Time is money in the door-to-door sales game.

This brings us directly to our next point. In order to notice the signs and signals that a potential buyer (or a non-buyer) sends you, sometimes you need to stop overthinking and be in the moment.

Don't Overthink Everything

Another experienced sales rep I looked to for motivation and knowledge provided me with another blurb about the door-to-door business. "This can be the easiest job in the world, or it can be the hardest job in the world. That choice is on you. Don't make it more complicated than it has to be. It's food in a box and everybody eats." That statement was so simple but so accurate.

At the core of my job was one simple mission. Find people who eat food, and give them a deal; nothing more, nothing less. But, unfortunately, in the door-to-door sales industry, sales reps tend to be their own worst enemies. Even the most successful door knockers get too wrapped up in specifics.

Sometimes they become too conscious of the territory they're working. One major downfall is the mindset that you've worked a particular area once, and it's not as good the second or third time around. Some guys get caught up about the neighborhood being too rich or too poor. I've seen reps get so inside their heads that they start blaming the color of the door on the end result of the sale or demo.

K.I.S.S. (Keep It Simple Stupid) is a term that's widely referenced in the sales industry as a whole; from car sales to mattress sales, gym memberships to meat, you'll see this written on wall-charts and dry-erase boards nationwide. But, as a new sales rep, it's hard to understand the relevance of a lot of the terminology if you have no background in the industry.

Tip #31. Don't overthink things too much. Keep everything simple in the field, and don't get in your head too much. It will ruin your day.

When we are in a slump or having a rough day, it's easy to blame our lack of production on external factors. However, the most beneficial move we can take in this situation is to look internally for a solution.

In door-to-door sales, you must put your blinders on. Stay focused on the goal, and don't let distractions and particulars slow you down. I'll use the frozen food industry I was in for the best example.

There's no secret to finding the "right house" or the "perfect customer." Do you know how you find your target demographic or individual? Knock doors, knock doors, and knock more doors. Every man, woman, and child on the face of this planet requires food to survive.

Let's say on any given day, even when I was working in a small town, there were 5,000 people at my disposal. The target demographic is any race, sex, religion, or ethnicity between the ages of 18 and 85. A great day ended with about five or six sales being made, and my profit would be anywhere from $400 to $700.

All I had to do was find five or six people out of 5,000 to buy a product from me that they already purchase on a daily and weekly basis as a means to survive. I had anywhere from six to ten hours to accomplish this goal.

When you put it in those terms, it really doesn't get any easier. Any door-to-door sale can be broken down to the most rudimentary terms, allowing for a clear picture of just how simple these positions are. But, unfortunately, it's the sales rep that makes them harder and overcomplicates things with assumptions staying locked in their head.

Tip #32. The numbers are in your favor. There are plenty of people to talk to. In most door-to-door sales industries, two to four sales are a successful day. That's not very much to muster up in the grand scheme of things.

When you are too fixated on your mind and take yourself out of the moment, it's nearly impossible to read customers and watch for the signs and signals they throw at you during an exchange. Likewise, in moments of anxiety or stress, you're too focused on being robotic or going through the motions that you miss the buying signs that are directly in front of you.

We will get more into detail about this later, but customers give body language and voice signals that let you know whether they are telling the truth, genuinely interested, or whatever the case may be. When you pay attention to these details, you can read between the lines and translate what a customer is really saying to you.

How is it possible to do this when you're locked in a battle of your mind? Focus on the customer and the goal at hand. Knock doors, pay attention to people and not circumstances, and knock on more doors.

Tip #33. Pay attention to a customer's body language, tone of voice, and what they're saying. It is one of the most critical elements of the sale. Again, customers will give you indicators and clues as to what they're really thinking through these actions.

The final tip builds on the one we just went over.

Don't Try to Convince or Oversell

This was a huge mistake that I made initially. Going back to the great first week I had and subsequent slump, this tip can be tied directly to that situation.

The first week was successful because the energy I put out could override any other element or potential setbacks. Then, after a couple of bad days, I was anxious and found myself scrambling to make money. Finally, I made the deadliest mistake a door-to-door salesman could; I tried to sell my customers the product.

At this point, I'm sure you're thinking, "Isn't a salesman supposed to sell?" My answer to this is no. A desperate salesman tries to sell you something. A good salesman makes you buy something by creating an inherent need for the product you have. The best salesman can demonstrate a problem you never knew you had and offer you the solution by purchasing their product.

Remember, the people you are talking to don't need your product. If they needed what you were selling, they would have called you for your services. You're a stranger intruding on their personal space, and the last thing they want to do is be sold anything.

Tip #34. Don't over-sell or overact when you're selling. People hate to feel like they're being sold to. Be natural and make normal conversation.

When you meet a potential customer, usually they decide if they like or trust you within the first 30 seconds. So the worst mistake you can make is to use these 30 seconds to try and sell them something.

If you're going to walk onto someone's doorstep or enter their yard, the best thing you can demonstrate is attention to their needs or wellbeing. Listen to what they have to say, and make a friend.

Your mission is to understand them and find out what their concerns are. Focus on them; the product is second. Once you know their story, you can get a clear picture of where their problem lies. After this, you can connect the dots and begin to offer them a solution.

You'll rarely get anywhere by convincing and trying to sell to a homeowner. Your product wasn't on their mind, to begin with. Try as you might, it's hard to sell someone anything they don't have the inherent need for. You can't offer a solution if they don't feel they have a problem.

Tip #35. Keep the focus on the customer. Make sure they feel like you're paying attention to their needs and concerns. It's important that a customer feels like you're trying to address their questions and concerns.

Keep all of these points in mind constantly throughout the day. As a beginner, I literally had to stop and remind myself of one or all of these points constantly during a workday. If you're not a sales veteran who understands the important, naturally occurring dynamics in the sale like the ones mentioned above, you'll need a reminder.

During my early days as a sales rep, I had to pull over and make a conscious effort to remind myself of these vital points. Failure to lose belief in the natural order and numbers game will lead to demoralization and feeling defeated.

Now that you understand some of the most crucial mindset points when you're knocking on doors, let's examine some of the external dynamics you have control over.

Dress for Success: Looking the Part

Many people would hear the term "dress for success" and assume it promotes a formal or professional office-style of attire. However, there are different ways to dress for success when working as a door-to-door sales rep.

What do we mean by this? Remember when I mentioned that you shouldn't convince or oversell when you are engaging homeowners? Well, this ties directly into that piece of advice.

For example, if you're selling cable or internet door-to-door, you're not going to choose the same attire as someone selling frozen steak and seafood door-to-door. When we knocked on doors in the steak and seafood industry, we wore laid-back attire. For example, in the fall and winter, I wore regular jeans, a hoodie (either a local college team hoodie or our company logo), and a pair of comfortable sneakers.

A cable or internet sales rep will usually dress in semi-business attire; typically, this consists of a polo shirt with the company logo tucked into a pair of dark slacks or khakis. A rep from a roofing company will also have more of a laid-back style of dress.

Tool salesman will not sport the business look while they are out working. Alternatively, a sales rep from an energy deregulation company will not knock doors in a t-shirt and jeans. You might be asking yourself, why such a stark contrast in how different reps dress from various industries?

A door-to-door sale is a sales rep playing a role from start to finish. Sometimes that role requires more acting than others. The perfect example of this was my position as a door-to-door steak and seafood salesman.

Keep in mind that the majority of my sales were from cold knocks each day. However, after six months to a year of working in the same area, I did establish several regular customers that bought different sized packages at varying times. Despite this, I would estimate that eighty percent of my sales were cold knocks.

However, I portrayed myself as a delivery driver that was expanding his route by bringing an extra product that day to give demos. These demo packages were available at a discounted cost for first-time customers. During the demo, we would show the customer a brochure that had packages priced around $300 and $400.

However, on that day, these customers could purchase these same packages for $169, $179, $200, or whatever price the customer agreed to in the end.

Tip #36. Dress according to the role you're playing as a salesman. Don't overdress or underdress for any position. Depending on your pitch, your attire should match your story.

The bottom line was I paid anywhere from $110 to $120 per case, and anything over that was mine to take home on every sale. I didn't end up getting top dollar for each package; at times, I sold them at cost, especially if there were volume or quota bonuses that day. My sense of urgency matched my attire.

When I showed up at the door as a delivery driver hungry to expand his route, people empathized with this. If I had been wearing a suit and tie, the whole picture I was painting would not have been nearly as realistic.

Chapter 3 Review

1. Maintaining a positive attitude is a significant key to success in door-to-door sales.
2. Get used to people telling you no; you'll hear no more than yes.
3. The faster you get to the no's, the quicker you get to a sale.
4. Don't overthink, and don't oversell.
5. Dress to match the role you're playing.

Chapter 4: The Most Important Rules to Remember in Sales

When people first begin selling any product door-to-door, generally, their focus is on the product, the deal, or something along those lines. I know that was the case for me. I spent hours researching the steak and seafood products I was selling, comparing other companies, and digging up everything I could that I thought would be good ammo to use during a sale. In my mind, the most crucial part was proving to a customer that our product was better and priced lower than any competitors.

It would have been relevant had they been calling me for my services. Because they weren't, those figures are the last things on a customer's mind. I also spent a great deal of time creating what I believed to be the perfect customer profile in my head. My opinion was that if I could go to a neighborhood that was upper class, if I had quality food for a better price, I would be sold out before I knew it. I also assumed that going to a lower-class neighborhood with food products for a deal would turn into an instant sellout. "Why haven't people thought of these things and done them before?" I asked myself.

The problem is, people have done these things before. Any idea I could conjure in my head, someone had already tried, and it probably wasn't the cash-cow they thought it would be. You see, the problem with most door-to-door sales reps (at least the new ones) is they try to reinvent the wheel. They enter the job with these preconceived notions and ideas of what they think will work and what won't. The truth is, it doesn't matter what you think. It didn't matter what I thought, and it won't matter what the next guy thinks. What works is what works.

Tip #37. Enter the job with a blank slate. You should come in ready to learn. It's good to have ideas, but don't let your assumptions stop you from learning essential basics.

I should have been mapping out entire areas and cities I wanted to hit and not being picky about specific neighborhoods. After coming out of my first slump, this is exactly what I ended up doing. I would start with a major state highway and turn down every road that intersected with this highway. I'd work either direction until I hit another major intersection, and I'd work my way back. I did this on either side of the highway. I stopped at every house that looked like it had signs of life. Keep in mind; I worked in the rural areas quite a bit. That's just my personal preference, and yours could be different. It isn't saying I never worked within city limits or bigger developments; I just preferred the country.

Tip #38. Cover everything when you work your territory. Don't be selective. Every house is a potential sale, so skipping certain homes or neighborhoods is ignoring money.

When I did make my way into a city, I worked the city blocks in a grid, picking through the area with a fine-tooth comb. I left no stone unturned. It is what I did when I was successful, after my slump. Before my rut, I thought I knew everything. My ideas were better, and I would do it better than anyone else had because I was smarter, which couldn't have been further from the truth.

On your first day, you need to remember three things. Door-to-door sales is a contact sport, your attitude is everything, and it doesn't matter where you work. These three things alone will bring you moderate success. You can know hardly anything about the product or the company you work for, and with these three things, you can build a door-to-door sales career. Obviously, you want to build on the other knowledge I mentioned, but don't overwhelm yourself initially. First, you need to learn the basic science of sales and play the numbers game.

Door-to-Door Sales is a Contact Sport

Anybody that has seen the movie Boiler Room might recognize this phrase. In the movie, they weren't referencing door-to-door sales; they were talking about phone sales. But the general idea is still the same. It can be said for almost any sales position that exists. Sales is a contact sport. What does this mean?

The more people you contact, the more successful you'll be. What I was doing by trying to find where the perfect demographic or customer lived was wasting time. It was precious time I could have spent knocking on doors and making money instead of pretending I knew what I was doing. In my defense, the things I assumed were pretty common sense. It isn't wrong to believe that a lower-class neighborhood might want a better deal on food. It isn't wrong to think a higher-class community would appreciate quality food at a quality price. The problem is, they just weren't in those buying modes.

Tip #39. The more people you contact, the more you're going to sell. This is true regardless of the product you are selling or the company you work for.

It is why you have to contact as many people as possible. After I was retrained and came out of my slump, I was like a whirlwind coming into a town. I would talk to everybody within a few feet of me. It didn't matter if I was at the gas station, getting lunch, in a neighborhood, in the country, in the woods; it literally didn't matter. Everybody was a potential sale to me, and I saw everyone with a dollar sign above their heads.

Since door-to-door sales (and any sales for that matter) is a numbers game, the higher your numbers are, the more chances you have of winning. Common sense tells you that if you need to sell a certain amount of product to hit a quota or make a specific dollar amount, the most direct pathway to this outcome is by talking to as many people as possible. So raise your odds, increase your chances, do what you have to do to speak to as many people as you can.

A lot of guys I worked around would do what's called "cherry-picking." Cherry-picking is when you knock on doors in a neighborhood or on a particular road, and you skip past the houses that don't look appealing to you. They would only stop and knock on the doors they thought looked like buying homes. I would always argue with these guys, telling them I had no idea you could tell what a person's eating habits were by the color of their door or the things in their yard. You never know what's going to be behind a door.

Tip #40. Don't become a cherry picker. A "cherry picker" is a salesman who hits doors that only he is drawn to because of the belief those specific doors are buyers.

I can't tell you how many times I knocked on a door that I wanted to skip, and it ended up paying huge dividends. Of course, I'm talking about the nastiest, rundown trailer you could ever imagine. Some of these places didn't even look livable, let alone have someone there with money to buy food. However, my assumption was wrong. On many occasions, I would sell my whole inventory to just one of these houses, walking away with $2,000 to $3,000 in profit. That was my money to take home. The total amount of the sale was anywhere from $4,000 to $6,000.

Do you know what made this possible? It wasn't because I was better looking or because I had a magic formula that showed me where the good houses were. It was because I treated the sales game like a contact sport, and I hit every door that got in my way. Had I been led by my assumptions and preconceived notions, I would have never picked that money up from the streets. It would have been left for the next man to find, and I probably wouldn't be writing this book right now.

Tip #41. There is opportunity behind every door. You never know how big of a sale could be waiting for you.

How many doors should you be hitting? In my opinion, you should be contacting anywhere from 50 to 75 people per day when you're new. As you progress through your career, this number will become lower, but when you're a rookie, focus on 50 to 75. If you're contacting 75 people in one day, it's not hard to get three to five of them to buy something from you. That's your goal. Find three to five people per day to like you and spend money with you, and you're golden. Normally this meets the quota regardless of the industry you're in.

This brings us to our next rule; attitude is everything in door-to-door sales. Anybody can go out and contact 75 people. However, getting those magic three to five people to like you is another story. Have you ever met people in life that just weren't likable? You can try as hard as you'd like, but you never seem to form a bond or any common ground with these people. They don't have many redeemable qualities and are just overall negative people.

Don't be that guy. I promise you; you won't find your magic three to five people by being that guy. Nobody will like you, which means nobody will buy from you, and your door-to-door sales career will be finished.

Tip #42. Talk to 50 to 75 people per day, and get three to five to buy. It is an excellent blueprint for success in door-to-door sales. Again, you should strive for this benchmark when you are new.

Attitude Is Everything

It could possibly be the most important rule in door-to-door sales. If you ask me, it's the most important rule regarding any type of sales. Your attitude is everything. The way you carry yourself and the level of positivity you operate with lays the groundwork for how successful you'll be in this business. If you don't start the day off with a good attitude, you might as well stop yourself and either readjust or take the day off. When you're working with a negative attitude, you're just wasting your time.

Tip #43. Don't carry a negative attitude with you into the field. It will kill your day 90% of the time. Positivity is the key to success.

Most people assume that sales are a transfer of money or a product. Truthfully, this is just a byproduct. A sale is a transfer of energy. The reason people buy from one person and not another is that they pick up on their energy, and it's contagious. For example, you can set two different salesman side by side with the same products, with one offering a higher price than the other. If the salesman with the higher price has a better attitude, he will make more sales than the rep with the cheaper price 90% of the time. I've seen it happen over and over again.

There were many days where I would work right behind another meat truck on the same road or in the same neighborhood. I would show up to doors an hour after them and sell to people who wouldn't even talk to them. It is because my attitude was in check. I was shining, and people wanted a piece of what I had (and I'm not talking about the food).

Tip #44. *A winning attitude beats out product knowledge and price every time. People gravitate towards a positive attitude. That's who customers want to buy from.*

I like to refer to it as a winning attitude. It's the same stuff that champions in sports or any winner in general has. When you're out in the field, you have to approach everything with a winning attitude with unmatched levels of motivation. You can't get mad when someone doesn't buy or doesn't look at your product. It's not for everybody; pack up and move on.

If you run into a rude customer, shrug it off. If there are problems at your house, leave them at home. You're not going to make any money arguing with your girlfriend, your wife, your parents, your brother, your sister, or anybody else over the phone while you're in the field. I used to turn my phone off while I was knocking on doors. I kept getting hung up on negative conversations or wasting time on social media. Eventually, my sales suffered, so I got the clue and shut it off. My numbers skyrocketed the next day.

One method that I used to keep my attitude in check each day and avoid getting negative has helped many sales reps. When I was at the door or in a house with a customer, I would always try to take something positive from the experience if they said no. It didn't matter if it was a nice comment, a bottle of water, a pen, a snack, a full meal, or anything else; I just wanted a positive takeaway. It does things for the subconscious mind like you wouldn't believe. Essentially, that's all sales are. It's a way of manipulating the subconscious mind to do things without directly suggesting or forcing that desired result. You use it on customers, and you should use it on yourself.

Tip #45. Having a positive takeaway from every door regardless of the outcome is a great way to keep you in a good place throughout the day mentally.

Even though I didn't make a sale at that house, my mind recognized the fact that I walked away from that door with something positive. It kept me going to the next door because I wanted more. I wanted that rush of positivity. It's almost like a drug for me when I'm out knocking on doors. That rush of positivity is addictive, and when you hit a big sale, there's nothing like it. The thrill of walking away with a profit of $3,000 or $4,000 after thirty minutes of your time is unexplainable. That's what I lived for in sales. The money was always a byproduct. I was chasing the feeling.

Does It Matter Where You Knock Doors?

After about six months of knocking on doors, one of my biggest problems was worrying too much about the area I was working. Believe it or not, after about six months of working in the same metro area, I felt like I had talked to everyone there was to talk to. I know it sounds ridiculous, but it happens to a lot of door-to-door salespeople. It's called becoming too territory conscious.

After you see the same roads and neighborhoods so many times, you feel like your chances of having success there are lower. It couldn't be further from the truth. I worked with guys that had been knocking on the same doors consistently for fifteen and twenty years, and they were still paying the bills. There's a saying in the door-to-door meat business that's extremely relevant in this situation. "It's never the land; it's the man."

Tip #46. It doesn't matter where you knock on doors. Everyone is a potential buyer. There are deals in every town, city, and neighborhood.

This statement would prove to be true over and over again in my sales career. You have to look at dynamics that are just plain old common sense. I began knocking on doors in the Portland, Oregon metro area. There are over a million people in the city and surrounding areas. In six months, there was no way I had even put a dent in the population. Somewhere in my mind, though, I was telling myself the area was burnt.

Anytime I ever hit a slump in the sales business, it was self-induced. It was never external for me; the problem was always internal. I had a way of psyching myself out like no other. Guys used to make fun of me for it. They used to tell me I thought about things way too much. So I guess I've always been an over-analyzer.

This can be a blessing and a curse in sales. Sometimes it paid huge dividends, and sometimes it kicked me in the butt. Most of the time, in door-to-door sales, you need to turn your blinders on. It's way too easy to lose focus thinking about all the "what ifs" and other questions that aren't relevant at the time. So instead, keep your eyes on the prize. The only relevant thing is the next door and who is behind it.

Tip #47. Don't kill yourself by worrying about "what if" questions. Just go with the flow, hit doors, talk to people, and make money. It's that simple.

It took me a couple of years to get over being too worried about the doors I was knocking. After I worked in Portland, Oregon, for six months, I met with the owner of the company, and he asked me if I'd be interested in managing for him. I quickly answered yes. We drove to our Seattle location, which was having problems at the time, and I checked things out. After a couple of days, I formally accepted and took over the office. I'm telling you this because there was a sales rep there by the name of Stan. Everyone called him Stan the Meat Man.

Stan helped me get over my problem of being overly concerned with the area I was working. This guy was somewhat of a legend in the Seattle area. He had been knocking doors and selling meat in the same area for about 25 years and was consistently the top rep every week. If someone took over the number one spot on the board, it's because Stan didn't work that week. This guy was a machine.

He wouldn't have monster days, but he was consistent. He was always a few sales above quota, and he did it every single day. I'm not exaggerating when I say I never saw this guy have a bad day. Instead, he was a brick wall of positivity and consistency.

The most amazing thing about Stan was that he never drove out more than 20 miles in either direction to knock on doors. Considering that some guys drive as far as two and three hours in one direction some days, this is incredible. I asked him one day how he did it. His answer was simple, but it really hammered things home for me. "Why would I ever drive out more than 25 minutes? There are five million people here. There are neighborhoods of every size and shape with all types of people, and they all eat." The simplicity of his statement hit me like a ton of bricks. Ever since that day with Stan, I didn't care about where I worked. You could drop me off blindfolded in any neighborhood in America, and I was going straight to work. It is another example of how keeping things simple in sales can benefit you in the end.

Chapter 4 Review

1. Contact as many people as you can to be successful (50-75 per day).
2. Don't skip houses or neighborhoods, and maximize your territory.
3. Sales is a transfer of energy, don't let the negative ruin the deal.
4. There's no need to reinvent the wheel; stick with what works.
5. There's a deal behind every door in every city, town, and neighborhood.

Chapter 5: Breaking Down the Process

In any sales position, there is a certain process from the initial contact to the point of sale. In door-to-door sales, this is the most critical part of the process. The reason the process is so crucial is that this is a cold sale. Specific language – spoken and body must be used to get the customer into buying mode. Their guard is up; they've never met you, so there's no trust, put yourself in their shoes.

From the starting moment, after you knock, you are a stranger at their door. You have about 10 seconds after they see you make an impact and get them to trust you. From that point, you have about 10-30 minutes to walk out with a check anywhere from $100-$3,0000 (or more). Anyone who can accomplish this is pretty powerful, wouldn't you agree? I'm going to show you how I did it.

Tip #48. Customers decide if they trust you in the first ten seconds. So make a good first impression – smile, shake your head yes, and use the correct body language.

The process is broken down into three sections – the knock (or hook), the demo (or show), and the close (the sale). So let's get into it.

The Knock

The knock is arguably the most crucial part of the entire process. Sure, the close gets you the money. But without a solid knock or hook, you will never get a chance to try and close them. It takes a strong personality to get through a door, considering you only have about ten seconds to get the customer to trust you. Let's outline the process step-by-step.

Step 1

Walk up to the door at a steady pace. I like to jog because it builds urgency, but do whatever feels right to you. When you get to the door, always knock; never ring the doorbell. Rarely do welcomed guests ever ring the bell, and we want to feel as welcomed as possible. So give a friendly knock without being too firm or overbearing. You don't want to sound like the police.

Tip #49. Step back 10-feet after you knock. Again, it's important to give the customers room, so they don't feel threatened.

Step 2

After you knock, take two or three big steps back. You want to have a reasonable distance between you and the customer so they don't feel threatened. Keep your hands out of your pockets and visible. Sometimes I would even turn my back to make me the vulnerable one. After they knock, give a smile and wave. Remember, positivity is the key.

Step 3

In an upbeat tone, go into your pitch. I'll use mine for this example.

"Hey, I'm sorry to interrupt you guys... I'm not sure if I had a chance to talk to you last time; I take care of some of the neighbors, they get food delivered. We do the wholesale steak and seafood variety packs (making a box shape with my hands). Anyway, whenever I'm out, and about I like to talk with all the neighbors and give them a chance to try everything for half price; it's just something we do to advertise; we usually give away a lot of free stuff, too. I know it's kind of a crazy question, but you guys eat steak, right?"

I'm talking with my hands the entire time, I'm using different tones in my voice, and I remember to stay positive and upbeat. Now, the ideal response is "yes, we do." In that case, I run to the truck, and I grab the product. However, it's not always an easy fight. Depending on what you're selling, there are different rebuttals. We will go into those in a separate chapter.

Tip #50. Nodding your head "yes" and saying things like "right" and "don't you?" will lead the customer into an agreement with you. It is very powerful.

There are a few important things to remember when you first knock on the door.

- Never talk to men and women the same. Never talk to older and younger people the same. Your tone of voice and what you say in the pitch will vary based on the target, but the core will remain the same. It's not what you say; it's how you say it.
- Always keep your hands visible.
- Always give them space when they open the door.
- Never ask them questions like "Would you be interested? Do you want to look? Would you like to buy?" The answer will always be no, guaranteed.

Now let's get into your demo or show. This one will be a little tricky since every demo is different depending on the product, but I'll give you the meat of the process to give you a good idea of how it goes down.

Tip #51. Use voice fluctuation and emphasize certain words like you would in a normal conversation. Don't talk to men and women the same. It's important not to sound robotic.

The Demo

The demo, also known as the show, is the second major step in the sales process. It is where you get a chance to enter the customer's home and give them a demonstration or allow them to look at whatever you are selling. It's important to keep in mind that when you do a demo, the ideal situation is being inside the customer's home. It is where they feel comfortable, and if they allow you inside the house, it means they have at least some form of trust for you.

Small details about the demo will change depending on what you're selling, but the basic idea and flow will remain the same. So I'll do a quick rundown of my demo for the steak and seafood business.

Tip #52. You should always be in the customer's house when you do a demo. It puts them in their comfort zone, and it usually means they trust you.

Step 1

After I walk up with the product, I get to their door and start wiping my feet. It subliminally tells the customer you are coming into the house. Then I ask them if they have a table where I can show them the product because I don't want to put their food on the ground. Throughout the whole process, I am constantly giving them a sense of ownership. I say "your food" or "your product." It makes them feel like it's already theirs.

Tip #53. Wipe your feet on a rug as you're walking up with the product you will demo. Subconsciously this tells them you're coming in the house, and their automatic response is to open the door and welcome you inside.

Step 2

When I get into the house, I ask the person I'm showing if they're capable of making a buying decision on their own. If they say yes, I continue. If they say no, I do more research, finding out who makes the decision and if there's any way around this. Then I ask for them to grab me a pen to open the case of meat. Finally, I might ask another person present, like a child, to grab me a glass of water. I don't really need these things, but it's all about taking control.

Step 3

The case of meat I sold had six boxes to a case. So basically, I'm opening six individual boxes and showing them separately as part of a set. While I'm doing this, I have a closing question I ask with each package. These are the questions I would ask:

- You guys have a little bit of freezer space, right?
- Where do you usually shop?
- You normally buy the groceries, right?
- How many people are you feeding?
- If I did something crazy, how would you guys pay? Cash, check, debit, or credit?
- If you tried the food and liked it, you could tell a few neighbors, right?

Tip #54. Ask closing questions throughout your demo. It gets them prepared to buy. You're subconsciously leading them into a sale.

Building Value

The most important part of the demo is building the value of your product. The customer has to clearly understand what the product is worth, why it's worth that amount, and why the price you are offering is a deal.

Build value, but don't romance the product. If you hype it up too much, the customer will feel like it's a gimmick, or you're too much like a salesman. It can turn a good sale bad fast.

When you build value, use real-life examples. Put your customer in the shoes of someone who is using the product. Make them feel like they need that product in their life. For instance, with steak, I would give them mental pictures of cooking it for their family or how easy dinner would be if they bought my product. Make them want it. Create a problem and have the solution.

Tip #55. Build value during the demo. You have to make the customer believe your product is worth the price you are offering. Don't overdo it, though; you don't want to give them the hard sell.

Taking Control

I touched on this earlier, but I can't stress the importance of taking control of the sale. It means leading the conversation and directing the momentum of the sale. So, for example, if a customer has an objection, you have to be able to respond with the right questions to take control of the direction of the exchange.

The customer should never have control. You want to ask them questions because they should have the feeling that you are genuinely trying to address their concerns and meet their needs. To them, it will seem like they have control, but in reality, you are directing the flow of things.

Sometimes if they start becoming negative about the whole idea of buying, you have to move the topic to another place. Start talking about something on their wall. Find common ground. Take them out of sales mode and cool them off; then, you can come back to the business at hand.

Tip #56. Taking control allows you to lead the momentum of the exchange the whole way. It's almost like you have mind-control over the customer, leading them into answering questions the way you want them to respond.

Asking the Right Questions

This goes back to my previous point of asking questions that only garner a yes answer. Ask things like:

- If the price was right, could you take advantage of the deal today?
- Do you guys like to save money?
- Do you know a good deal when you see it?
- Would you call yourselves intelligent consumers?
- Is saving money important to you?
- If I could show you a product you could use at a great value, could you use it today?

Asking questions like this will get you a yes answer 99% of the time. You want to lead up to the close with nothing but yes answers. It is extremely helpful when it's time to ask for the money.

This leads me to the close of the sale.

Tip #57. Part of taking control is asking the right questions. Of course, you want to ask questions that you know will only garner a yes response or the response you want.

The Close

Step 1

After showing them all the food, I pulled a brochure out that showed a "retail" price for the cases of meat. Most door-to-door sales will have some type of tool like this. It will show a regular price for the product you have so you can hit them with a better deal to give them an incentive to buy from you at that exact moment.

Step 2

The brochure would say the steak case was $399. I would tell them at $399 for the whole case, and it works out to about $10 per steak. That's about what you pay at the grocery store, right? As I'm saying this, I'm nodding my head, "yes." It gets them to agree with you; 90% of the time, they agree. Immediately afterward, I tell them, "well, if you guys help me out with one case today, we're giving new customers another whole case of their choice for free. That works out to about $4 to $5 per steak. That's way better than the store, right?" Nine times out of ten, they agree and say yes.

Step 3

After they agree and say yes, I start closing them. I immediately ask, "which freezer should I put it in? and you guys said you were paying with a credit card, right? I'll go grab you a receipt!" I run back to the truck as fast as I can and grab the paperwork. It's crucial they don't have a lot of time to themselves. A door-to-door sale is sensitive, and you want to be in control the whole time. Every minute you're away a minute you're not in control.

Tip #58. One of the most powerful closing questions you can ask is, "If the price was right how would you take care of this today, cash, check, debit, or credit?"

When you're closing a deal, the most important thing to remember is to ask questions that will automatically garner a yes response. You don't want them to answer no to anything. The whole point of this technique is once you get them in the habit of saying yes when you ask for the sale, the answer is an automatic yes. A sale is all mental, with most of the work done in a customer's subconscious mind.

A good door-to-door salesperson will get a customer to do what they want without even asking them. They won't even know they are getting sold. That's the point you want to get to. That's when you're unstoppable.

After the sale is closed, there should be no more extra talk beyond business. You've already gotten them to trust you, so you don't need to show that extra personality. Now it's time to get down to business. I've seen plenty of salespeople lay it on too thick after the close, and they talk themselves right out of the deal. Once they've committed, get them to sign, get the payment, and wrap it up.

Asking for the Money

When it comes to closing a deal, new salespeople have a problem with asking for the money. Remember, just because a customer is closed doesn't mean the deal is done. You have to ask for the money.

I can't tell you how many times I've seen a customer closed – done deal, food in the freezer, everything is unpacked...and the rep doesn't know how to ask for the money. During the middle of my show and at the end, I asked them how they would pay if the price were right. Let's say they indicated that they would pay with a check. Then, after they are closed and agree to the deal, I would say something like:

- "Okay, you guys said you were paying with a check, right? Let me grab you a receipt."
- "What freezer did you guys want this in? I'll start packing it away, and then I'll grab you a receipt."
- "How do you guys usually pay for your food?
- (Customer response)

- "Okay, I'll go get the receipt book."

Sometimes it was just as simple as saying, "Okay, I'll go get the receipt book." But, you can close someone and lose the sale by not asking for the money. Rarely will a customer volunteer to initiate a payment transaction. But, it does happen – MAYBE 10% of the time.

Tip #59. You have to ask for the money. A closed deal can be blown by not asking for the money the right way or at the right time.

Closing the Deal Tight

At the very end of the process, you have to make sure the deal is closed tight. What do I mean by this? It means you have to close the deal tight, so there's no customer service or buyer's remorse.

Buyer's remorse is the number one reason for cancellations In the door-to-door sales business. People end up writing a salesman a check, and twenty minutes later, they come back to their senses, wondering why they just made a purchase for $2,000 to a stranger at their door. They panic, or their spouse gets mad, and next thing you know, they're calling the 1-800 number to cancel. It means you can kiss all that commission you just made goodbye.

You don't want commission deductions, so it's important to close your deals tight. There are several ways to ensure this takes place.

- Cool the customer off. After you get payment, talk with them for 10-15 minutes. At this point, you can joke with them again, maybe have a more personal conversation. Solidify the fact that you're their friend. We will get into this more in the following chapter.

- Show them the company website, assuming you have one. Go over ways they can get help if they ever need it. Let them know the company handles customer service.
- Make sure they have a copy of the receipt and include your number and the company number.

The basic idea here is not just to dash out the door. It leaves a bad taste in their mouth. They feel like they just dealt with a fly-by-night company. Taking this extra 10-15 minutes at the end of every sale will cut down your cancellations and customer service substantially.

Tip #60. Closing the deal tight ensures you have almost zero customer service calls or cancellations.

Chapter 5 Review

- When you knock on the door back up, give them some space, and show them your hands.
- Smile, nod your head, and have a good attitude.
- During your demo, take control and build value.
- Only ask "yes" questions during the demo and close.
- Ask for the money and close the deal tight.

Chapter 6: After the Dotted Line is Signed

When a door-to-door sale is finalized, this doesn't signify the end of the process by any means. Instead, there are several steps a rep should take at the end of a sale to cool the customer off and later ensure the customer is satisfied.

Customers that buy are a great place to obtain leads for new sales as well. We'll cover all of these steps and more in this chapter. Step-by-step, we'll outline the post-sale process that lowers your customer service and cancellation rate and can garner you more money in the form of referrals. First, we'll start with how to cool a customer down.

Cooling Down Your Customer

After every sale is finalized, it's vital to spend an extra 10-15 minutes with them to help cool them down. A door-to-door sale happens very fast, almost too fast for a customer to even comprehend what's going on. They're so focused on what you're saying that it's hard for them to analyze everything until after you leave. It's almost like your subconscious power of suggestion hypnotizes them. That's a term that was used for a lot of good sales reps. "It's like they're hypnotizing people out there!" In a sense, we were.

Tip #61. It's essential to take 10-15 minutes to cool the customer down. It lowers your cancellation rate.

During the cool-down period, you will go over the sale details with the customer, ways to get in touch with you later, and a few other essential elements. When you do this, they can get a better grasp of what just happened. The questions start hitting them after a salesman leaves. So it is when buyer's remorse happens (if it does happen). It makes sense to field all of their questions while you're there proactively instead of doing it defensively when they call later.

Below is a list of things to go over with the customer after the deal is closed and payment has been taken.

- Use their copy of the receipt and go over everything they just purchased. For example, when I sold steak and seafood door-to-door, I would go over the amount of each type of meat they ordered, how much it was, and the price-per-serving one more time. If I packed the freezer, I'd tell them where everything was as a reminder.
- Show them where they can find your phone number and the company phone number on the paperwork. Our products were guaranteed for an entire year, so I always circled the guarantee and phone number and told them exactly how to handle any questions. I never used the word complaints. I simply told them all questions could be directed to my cell phone number or the company number.

Tip #62. Go over the sale details, how they can have their concerns addressed, and how they can reorder.

One thing I liked to do was call them immediately after leaving the house. I would wait until I was about five minutes up the street, then I'd stop and call them. The call would go something like this:

"Hey, it's the steak and seafood guy. I'm sorry to interrupt you guys again. I just wanted to call you from my cell phone number to make sure you guys had it. I also wanted to say thanks again for helping me out. If you guys need anything at all, don't hesitate to call this number. Next time I'm in the area, I'll be sure to stop in and say hello."

You wouldn't believe something as simple as this two-minute phone call does for customer service rates and repeat business. It gives you credibility. It shows customers you're not hiding from them, and you're available at all times if they need assistance. In all of my years as a door-to-door salesman, this was one of my most powerful tools.

Tip #63. Making a quick two-minute phone call right after you leave the house can be a great way to build more trust between you and the customer. It gives them more confidence in the ability to contact you if they need anything further.

Asking for Referrals

After cooling a customer down, I would always ask for referrals. I would strategically do this right before exiting their home. Then, as I was getting ready to turn the knob and leave, I'd look back and say, "I almost forgot. Do you guys know any nice people around here who could use the same type of deal I gave you?" The reason for doing it this way was to take any urgency away from me asking the question. I didn't want to seem desperate, so nonchalantly doing it is the best way to get this information.

Normally, people will always send you referrals. I would tell them if they could give me five solid referrals, I would give them a discount on their next order. It just gives them extra incentive to really think of someone worthwhile who could actually buy.

Tip #64. Ask your customer for four solid referrals before exiting the home. It can lead to easier sales with people who already have some knowledge about you. In addition, some trust is already built considering one of their friends or family members just purchased from you.

Did all of these people end up purchasing? No, not even close. However, I can say that about 30% of them did, which is huge. Those are people I wouldn't know about otherwise, and it made my day much easier. You also already have a rapport with these people because someone they trust just did business with you.

It's important to note the difference between solid referrals and just nonsense a customer is throwing out there. If you know how to read people, you should have a good understanding of whether they are pulling your leg or not. In case you don't, here's a list of things to look and listen for.

- If they give you a name and address and go into details about where the house is, they are probably a solid lead. It shows they put some thought into making sure you know where the house is.
- If they sound unsure about it or hesitate to give you any leads at all, they're probably just giving you random names.
- When they call someone, usually, you can count on it being a solid lead. If the person doesn't answer, go there anyway.
- When they do get someone on the phone, don't try to sell them over the phone. Just give a short pitch and tell them you're on the way. You want to be able to put the product in front of them and make the magic happen in person.

Tip #65. Knowing the difference between a solid referral and a customer just giving you a random name is essential. You don't want to waste your time chasing something that won't pan out.

One significant thing to remember is making sure customers don't mention the prices they paid to one another. If they paid the same price for the same deal, it's not an issue. However, if one got a better deal than the other, tell them to keep the amount to themselves. It can create customer service problems later if they call each other to talk about the deals they purchased. I've had this happen before, and you always end up losing money.

Tip #66. It's important to tell customers not to communicate the prices they paid to one another if they didn't get the same deal.

Something else that's very important to remember when you deal with a referral is having a reason to drop your price. If customer A tells customer B what they paid, and you end up giving it to customer B for a low cost, always have a good reason why. Tell them you had extra inventory, and you can discount some. Tell them you have some promo or sample items, and these are available for less. Tell them you earned some product as a bonus, and you're doing it for a much lower price. Whatever the reason is, make sure you have a purpose behind lowering the cost. Otherwise, they're going to think you're full of crap, and it might blow both sales. Keep it professional, don't just throw prices around like a used car salesman.

Tip #67. Always have a reason to drop your price. Randomly dropping your price with no solid reason behind it makes you seem somewhat shady.

First Contact After the Sale

Many of the sales reps that I worked with during my career were afraid to hit repeat customers. I was famous for repeat business and upselling. After closing a sale, I would go back to the truck like I was leaving. I would go back and knock on the door and tell them I had a couple of extra packs on the truck I forgot about, and if the price was right could they help me out with them.

The easiest person to sell is the person you just sold. That is something fundamental to remember when you're selling. Now I want to get into first contact after the sale, and I don't mean upselling. I'm talking about a genuine repeat customer you hit a few months after they buy initially.

Tip #68. Don't be afraid to upsell your customers. The easiest person to sell is the one you just sold.

The only reason a salesperson should be scared about hitting a repeat customer is if they used shady tactics the first time. Sometimes reps feel that a door-to-door sale is a one-shot deal, which isn't true at all. I knew Kirby Vacuum sales reps who have sold one-person multiple vacuums. Remember, door-to-door sales are never about the product; it's about you. People buy because they like you.

When you go back to a repeat customer and attempt to sell them again, you should use close to the same pitch as last time. The reason for this is because if it worked once, it would work again. Don't even mention they bought from you until you get the product in the house. Honestly, I treated every repeat customer at the door like it was a fresh knock. I never knocked and acted like I was familiar with them. I used the same urgency as before and the same pitch.

After I got into the house, I would mention subtle things like, "you guys remember these from last time, right?" It always seemed to work better. Door-to-door sales is a very strange profession in the sense of customer behavior. I think it's because the people who buy get a particular rush from buying just as we get a thrill from the sale. It's exciting to them, so it's essential to give them this same feeling when you return. They like the feeling of a surprise bargain they can jump on.

Tip #69. Approach repeat customers the same way you did when you sold to them initially. If it worked once, it would work again.

Make some sort of filing system for all of your receipts. Keep a journal with your sales and log the customer's name, address, phone number, and whatever they purchased. It helps you have a better idea of what ballpark to pitch in the next time you go back and attempt to sell them. That's another thing about door-to-door sales. Most of the time, repeat customers will buy almost precisely what they bought before. The price may vary by a hundred dollars or so, but customers always seemed to stick within the same comfort zone regarding price.

Once in a blue moon, I could hammer a huge deal on someone that was a small buyer in the past. These situations were rare and usually ended up being a one-time deal. Typically, if I went back a third time, they would return to their initial, more modest scale.

Tip #70. Keep a solid filing system for your receipts so you can keep track of all of your customers and try to sell them again.

Customers rarely called me to reorder food. I had a few very loyal, unique customers that did, but this was very rare. Normally, I would always have to show back up and knock on the door. I never could figure out a reason for this. I always wondered if they liked the food and thought it was a deal, why didn't they ever call back? I guess that buying this way was so different from their regular routine that they just went back to the grocery store afterward. I think that, and also the fact that usually, they would have to spend such a large amount with me ($400 or more, which is some people's budget for the month), that it was hard for them to willingly pick up the phone and commit to this type of purchase.

I would learn later that this was the case. The reason companies like Omaha Steaks had such a large following is because they sold smaller quantities. Our packs were huge, and usually, a customer had to spend at least $200 to get anything from me. Regardless, it's always good practice to go see your customers face-to-face the second time around. It's more personal, and it's easier to make the sale.

Tip #71. Never attempt to sell your customer over the phone. Face to face is the only way in door-to-door sales.

Chapter 6 Review

1. Always cool your customer down before leaving.
2. Make some sort of phone contact with them after the sale.
3. Ask for referrals before you leave, and make sure they're reliable.
4. Keep track of your sales so you can go back and sell them again.
5. Always contact them face-to-face when attempting to make them a repeat customer.

Chapter 7: Tips and Tricks from a Door-to-Door Expert

Now that you've been given the essentials for selling door-to-door, you can digest some additional tips and tricks to help you with your success rates. However, the most important thing to keep in mind is the very thing I've been stressing the entire duration of this book. Door-to-door sales (and any sales in general) is an entirely mental game.

The product only has a portion of the influence on the direction of the sale. The majority of the outcome lies in the personality of the salesperson and their ability to lead the customer in the direction of a purchase. Once you understand these key elements, you can start to become a power closer.

The first thing I'll touch on in this section is mirroring your customer. It is imperative when it comes to how comfortable a customer is and how well they mesh with you. Mimicking your customer doesn't mean you will act entirely like them, but you will mirror some of their most significant mannerisms. Let's get into it more.

Mirroring Your Customer

Mirroring your customer is a process that involves you matching a customer's mannerisms and nuances during a verbal exchange. Why is this important? People see other people as they see themselves, so naturally, a person is comfortable with someone who has the same nuances as they do. So what are the traits you want to match?

- If a person has a lower tone of voice, you should respond with a softer tone of voice. The last thing a soft-spoken person wants is for someone to bark back at them with a loud, hyper pitch.
- Likewise, return the same energy if someone is coming at you with a loud, confident persona. These people often act out of intimidation, and it's essential that you show you can't be intimidated. These customers will try to beat you down during a sale to get a lower price. So you have to keep up with them every step of the way.
- When someone talks with their hands more than usual, mirror them in the same way.

Tip #72. Mirror your customer and match their mannerisms. It makes them feel more comfortable.

Many salespeople that I worked with would often be afraid of dealing with a loud, boisterous customer. It's not hard to picture the type I am talking about. It's the type of person who thinks they know better than everyone, have more knowledge and know-how than most people, and can do everything better. You know the personality type who I'm talking about.

People like this didn't scare me away. In fact, I would seek out people like this. The reason is that if you can speak their language and show them, you're not intimidated; these can be the biggest fish you can find in the field. If you can verbally and mentally go pound-for-pound with someone like this and match wits with them, chances are they're going to be a big buyer.

Tip #73. Loud, confident customers shouldn't intimidate you. If you know how to handle them, they can be big buyers.

They're just looking for the right person that can fulfill their requests and needs as a buyer. They have a high opinion of themselves, so it's impressive to them when you can match that.

Rarely do they meet someone whose information they feel they can rely on. But when they do, they don't shy away from pulling their wallet out. Generally, people with a comfortable amount of money fit this profile. They're very successful in life and aren't afraid to tell people about it.

This is a perfect example of why mirroring your customer is so important. For some reason, mentally, people are just comfortable with people they can relate to themselves. Don't forget that when you're in the field, as it can garner you substantially higher close ratios.

Tip #74. Match their energy and meet the requirements they have as a customer, and you usually can take them down.

Handling Objections

One of the most important parts of your job as a door-to-door salesperson will be knowing how to handle objections. I was going to include this portion of the book in the chapter outlining the knocking, demo, and closing steps, but I felt it needed its own section.

Below, I've outlined some of the most common objections and ways to rebuttal them. For some of them, I've included information specific to steak and seafood sales.

Granted, each separate sector of door-to-door sales is different as far as objections go. However, most of these examples can be plugged into any particular industry and work just the same. You might need to adjust them slightly depending on what you're selling, but they are relatively universal.

Tip #75. Most objections are universal regardless of the type of product you are selling door-to-door. Pay attention to what customers say specifically and give them proper acknowledgment.

1. *I have to wait until my husband/wife gets home.*

"I understand that, and it's a very considerate thing for you to do. However, I'm sure your husband/wife has trusted you to make important decisions before, right? I mean, they wouldn't have married you if they didn't trust your judgment. Plus, this is something practical that's a need, not a want. So I'm sure this is something they would agree needs to be taken care of."

Tip #76. The "husband/wife isn't home" objection is usually the most common. It is also the easiest to rebuttal.

2. *I'm not sure if we can afford it. I have to wait until my husband/wife gets home.*

"Well, you have to look at it like this. Sure, it's a little more upfront than what you're used to spending on your grocery budget at one time. If your electric company offered you nine months for free if you paid three upfront, you'd probably jump on it, right? This is the same exact situation, but with your food. The money you're taking out of your front pocket goes right to your back pocket."

3. *We haven't tried your product before.*

"I know, if you were regular customers, you would have called me, right? We have a very reputable website, and all of our products are backed by a one-year guarantee, so there's nothing to lose. It's better to try something and know for sure than to have wondered

if you missed out on a good opportunity. It's only a deal if you take it."

4. We would like to think about it. We haven't tried your product before.

"It's good to think things out and make informed decisions. That's why I've spent so much time in here with you, to show you the value of our product. What else are you concerned about that I can help you with?"

5. Someone we know tried your company before and didn't like the product.

"Are you sure it was our company? It would be helpful if your friend could recollect the name of the company because I'm certain it wasn't ours. We handle all of our customer service and rarely get complaints. If it was our company, I'd like to know so we can rectify the situation. With a one-year guarantee, it's hard for anyone to have a bad experience. You can check our Better Business Bureau rating."

It's important to note here that most of the time, it wasn't your company the customer had a bad experience with. It is because there are so many door-to-door sales companies out there; the chances of it being yours are slim to none. So, assuming you work for a reputable company, this is the best response to use.

Tip #77. If someone says they didn't like the product or know someone who didn't, make sure it's your company specifically they are talking about.

6. Can you come back later?

This can be a tricky one to deal with. Sometimes, it pays to come back later because the decision-maker will be home. But, sometimes, they could just be trying to get rid of you.

"I can appreciate the fact you want the decision-maker here for the process. Are you certain this is something they would be interested in talking about? I would absolutely come back, but it would make me feel better if you called them, just so I know I'm not wasting their time or mine. I'm sure you can understand that, right?"

You will likely encounter many more objections, all of which you have to deal with individually. Of course, every customer is different, but these should give you a good start. Assuming you work with a good company, they should provide you with a training manual covering various forms of objections and the rebuttals you can use to overcome them.

Tip #78. Make sure that returning to a customer is worth it. One of the worst things you can do is waste time chasing deals that don't pan out.

Boxing Them In

Boxing a customer in is a term that refers to tying a customer down so they have no more objections. There are two basic ways to handle a sale. You can wait until the end to field their doubts, or you can use the boxing method, also known as the tie-down method. I'll give you an example of an exchange where I would box a customer in during a food sale. It takes place during the demo.

Tip #79. Boxing a customer in refers to a sales strategy where you eliminate objections before they arise.

Me: *"These are your 16 oz. T-Bones. You guys have a little freezer space to put something like this, right?"*

Customer: Yes, I believe we do.

Me: *"These are 12 oz. Ribeye. You guys would use these if you had them, right?"*

Customer: Absolutely.

Me: *"These are your 6 oz. chopped steak burgers. You guys use ground beef, right?"*

Customer: Yes, all the time.

Me: *"Good, you can use these for any ground beef recipe, or just use them for burgers since they're already formed that way. These are your 8 oz. Sirloin strips. If you guys really liked the food, you could tell a few neighbors about me, right?"*

Customer: Yeah, we wouldn't mind.

Me: *"Finally, these are your center-cut filets. If the price was right, you guys said you would probably pay with cash, right?"*

Customer: Yes.

Me: *"Okay, great, I'll go grab a receipt."*

Tip #80. Use this script to box customers in. Make minor adjustments if you need to, but this general outline will get the job done.

The reason for using the box-in method is that it takes away all of their objections before they can use them. Thus, you're addressing all of their concerns before they can voice them. It is why it's so important to ask questions throughout your exchange with a customer.

Asking these questions gives you a better idea of how to box them in. The more ammo you have, the higher your chances are of closing the sale. Obtaining as much information as you can is vital for the closing portion of the sale.

Tip #81. Boxing a customer in will increase your closing rates substantially. So master this art and watch your sales rise.

Chapter 7 Review

1. Mirror your customer to make them feel more comfortable.
2. Don't let a loud-talking customer intimidate you. Stand your ground.
3. Handle objections with the correct rebuttal. It's essential to use proper acknowledgment.
4. Box your customers in and increase your odds of closing a sale.
5. Ask questions to learn the most efficient way to eliminate objections.

Chapter 8: Tracking Your Success

In door-to-door sales, it's important to keep track of your success so you can grow as a sales rep. For example, if you don't know your door hooking ratio, you can never get better at hooking doors. Likewise, if you don't understand your close ratio, you'll never get better at closing.

What's the best way to go about this? First, you have to keep track of everything on paper. Designing a score sheet can help you keep track of and manage what your numbers are on a daily basis. It allows you to calculate your percentages, and from there, you can evaluate and see precisely where you need to improve.

Tip #82. Keep track of everything on your sales days. The more data you have, the more you can analyze and improve your technique.

Below, I've outlined the way I used to create my score sheet and track numbers. I think this is a pretty efficient way to do it, but you can make minor changes depending on what suits you the best.

Keeping a Score Sheet

The first thing you should do is grab a notebook that you designate solely for keeping score sheets. You can separate each day on a different page and then break your week down. It is also a rough way to keep track of customers as well. You can take the data written on your score sheets and build a proper filing system for your customers by using your score sheets and receipts.

Tip #83. Keep a score sheet to calculate your hooking ratio and your closing ratio.

- Use a journal and date the top of each page according to your days worked.
- When you hit a door, make a "/" mark that signifies each house you knocked on.
- If they answer, make an "X." If nobody answered, I would turn the slash into a "D," which stood for "dead door."
- When someone answered, if that door hook turned into a show, I would circle the X.
- For each show that turned into a sale, I would put a checkmark through the X and circle and write the information on the sale directly beneath it. For example, I would include the customer's name, address, what they bought, how they paid, and how much they paid.
- If the show didn't garner a sale, I would simply leave the circle with the X through it.

Tip #84. Keep track of every door hit, every demo you do, and every sale you close. Write down the information about each deal.

With the data you've collected, you can efficiently tally up your **door hook percentage**. First, count the number of doors you hit and successfully talk with someone. Don't count the dead doors. Then calculate the number of demos you did. Finally, divide the total number of doors where you made contact by the number of demos, and you have your door hook percentage. Anything between 20 and 30 percent is average and means you're doing your job. However, if you are above 30, it means you're a pretty powerful door hooker.

Tip #85. A good door hooking percentage is 20-30.

If you are below 20, find out what you're doing wrong and correct it. It could be something as simple as mixing up a few words or talking with your hands more.

You will calculate your **close ratio** in the same manner. However, to do this, you will add up the number of demos you did. Divide this by the number of successful sales, and you have your close ratio. A decent close ratio is anywhere from 40 to 50 percent. It could dip down to 30 when you're new, and as time goes on, it should steadily rise.

Tip #86. A good closing percentage is 50 percent.

If you are above 50 percent, you are approaching power closer status. Keep up the excellent work, and continue to perfect your craft. Never stop learning or growing.

This is an effective tool to use, especially when you are new. It allows you an in-depth view of what areas need improvement. It can be vital when you are in a slump as well. It can tell you if your hook needs improving or your close needs work. You can't fix yourself if you don't know what areas you lack in.

Tip #87. If you are above fifty percent, consider yourself a power closer, but never stop learning.

How Do I Measure Success?

I left this as the last section in the book for a good reason. Of course, it's essential to measure your success in sales, but something important should be noted. What you consider success and what someone else deems success could be two entirely different things.

Your numbers always measure success in the office. However, numbers aren't what I'm talking about here. I'm not even necessarily talking about money. Sure, money gets us the things we require, but it's not the final measurement for what makes us successful for some people.

What I mean by this is it's important to find your 'why.' Why do you get up early every day and knock on doors? Why do you strive to be the very best you can be every day?

Tip #88. You can measure your success by finding your 'why.'

For me, it was my two children. I have two beautiful daughters that mean the world to me, and failure was never an option. Failing meant not giving my daughters the things they needed and wanted in this life, and that couldn't happen.

Being successful meant giving every day 110% regardless of the outcome. Even on days where I didn't hit my money or numbers goal, I felt better at the end of the day, knowing I gave it 110%. I left everything in the field and exhausted every resource I had to get the job done. On the days where I didn't hit my money or numbers goal, it hurt. But knowing I gave it my all took the sting away.

Tip #89. Give it 110% all the time. You will be more fulfilled and feel better about your hard work regardless of the outcome of your day.

It all goes back to setting goals and rewarding yourself. To measure success, you must reward yourself in some way. Even if almost every dollar you make goes towards someone you love or even bills, it's important to hold back a little for yourself so you don't get burnt out. You have to see the fruits of our labor. I want to leave you with a shortlist of tips regarding goals and rewards.

- You should always reward yourself after a good day. If you hit your money and numbers goals, get yourself something to reward your hard work. It doesn't have to be extravagant or expensive. Each day I hit my goals, I rewarded myself with a more expensive cup of coffee from my favorite coffee shop.

Tip #90. Give yourself a small daily reward. It can be something as simple as a new pen or journal, as long as it's something.

- In the same fashion, it's also essential to have a monthly reward. Your monthly reward can be something more substantial. For example, I'd get myself something like a nicer pair of shoes I could use in the field to make my days more comfortable. But I had to hit my goals first. No goals, no reward.
- I know I touched on this earlier, but break your goals into smaller, more manageable goals. For example, have a daily, weekly, monthly, and yearly plan. It avoids discouragement and makes everything more achievable.

Tip #91. Give yourself a monthly reward as well. Break your goals down into small, achievable increments.

- Don't make your goals unrealistic. Set goals you know you can hit. Push yourself some, but don't make them impossible.
- Review your goals as often as you'd like. Put them in someplace you will look at them often. For example, I taped my goals to my rearview mirror in my truck. That way, every time I felt down, I went to look at myself in the mirror and saw my goals right there. I also had a picture of my two daughters beside them.

Tip #92. Make your goals realistic and review them often.

- Accountability is the most critical part of the job. Hold yourself accountable for your success and your failures. The only person you have to answer to is you.
- When you don't hit a goal, don't consider it a failure. Instead, consider it a chance to become better. The only time you truly fail is when you fail to try.

Tip #93. Hold yourself accountable at all times.

Quick Thoughts On Improvement and Not Hitting Goals

When you don't hit your goal, don't beat yourself up over it. Everybody fails to meet their goals in this world. But it doesn't mean you failed altogether. On the contrary, not hitting a goal gives you a chance to improve as a sales rep.

In my opinion, the days that I didn't hit my goals made me stronger. I am thankful for my hard days and see them as a blessing. If you aren't hitting your goals, consider using the following pointers to get back on track.

Tip #94. Sometimes not hitting your goals makes you stronger than meeting them. It's a chance to become better.

- If you don't hit your goals, analyze where you lack with the data you collected from the score sheet.
- Maybe your goals need to be broken down into smaller increments. It could be possible you are setting your goals too high. Put them to a more achievable level.

Tip #96. Not hitting your goals means you need to set more achievable ones.

- Don't be afraid to ask for a coworker's help. It always helps to go with a partner for the day to build back up your positive attitude.
- Become a student of the game and master your craft. Studying your technique is the best way to learn about yourself. You can explore what other people do as much as you want. However, analyzing what you do is the only way you're going to get better personally.

Tip #97. Don't be afraid to ask to go out with a partner and work to feed off of their momentum and positive attitude. Sometimes that's all it takes to get back on track.

Closing Thoughts

Door-to-door sales can be an incredibly tough industry. However, it's also gratifying. Unfortunately, only a small percentage of the population makes it in door-to-door sales. It is why the turnover rate is so high.

Tip #98. Those who are tough enough to make it in door-to-door sales get a large portion of the pie.

You have to have thick skin and be self-motivated. You have to be able to keep yourself positive. You have to manage money well. You literally are the owner, manager, employee, and accountant all in one. It can be an incredibly stressful position to hold at times.

However, for those who can manage it, a large piece of the pie is the reward. There is no intermediary in the supply chain for door-to-door sales. That's why the commission percentages can be so high. There's not a lot of overhead, and the product goes straight from the manufacturer to the consumer. You are the middleman.

Tip #99. The commissions are so high because we cut out the middleman.

When you become a door-to-door sales rep, people might look at it as an odd job. They might even tell you that it's not a real job. Disregard what everyone says. If you feel secure in your ability to complete the job efficiently and make a good living while doing it, carry on with business. Put your blinders on, and don't let what other people say bring you down.

Remember to keep learning and listening constantly. Never stop growing or becoming a sponge for knowledge. The moment you stop growing is the moment you start dying. Even the most successful door-to-door salesmen with years under their belt continue to grow and learn new things daily.

Tip #100. Ignore what everyone says and stay focused on your goals.

Keep your why in mind, and don't forget your goals. Stay positive and remember that every no brings you closer to a yes. I'll leave you with one challenge before I wrap up.

I challenge anyone knocking on doors to try something new during their next workday. Try something you've never tried before. For example, hit a different street or a new town. Knock on doors you wouldn't usually knock on. Hit businesses instead of houses and vice-versa.

It's important to continue to think outside of the box. Don't attempt to reinvent the wheel but push yourself to get uncomfortable and look for new ways to be successful. One of the best pieces of advice I ever had pertains to what I just mentioned.

Tip #101. Think outside the box, and don't be afraid to become uncomfortable.

"You will know when you are starting to grow as a salesman when the things you are doing and methods you are using make you uncomfortable. They might even hurt. But after the pain – after walking through the fire – there is new growth. That's how we become the best version of ourselves."

Chapter 8 Review

1. Keep a score sheet to monitor your progress.
2. Calculate your door hooking percentage and your closing percentage.
3. Remember 20-30 percent on hooking and 40-50 percent on closing.
4. Reward yourself on a daily and monthly basis.
5. Find your why that drives you to be successful. Then, measure your success with your 'why.'

About the Expert

The author of this HowTo guide is a veteran door knocker of ten plus years in the door-to-door sales industry. He has done everything from taking on the job of a national trainer, managing sales offices, and even owning his own door-to-door sales company. As a result, he is well-versed in the world of sales and is ready to pass on these mental tools of the trade to you.

Ten years in the door-to-door industry can give someone a lifetime of wisdom and firsthand knowledge. His veteran involvement with this industry makes him well-qualified to help any reader who picks up this book.

HowExpert publishes quick 'how to' guides on all topics from A to Z by everyday experts. Visit HowExpert.com to learn more.

Recommended Resources

- HowExpert.com – Quick 'How To' Guides on All Topics from A to Z by Everyday Experts.
- HowExpert.com/free – Free HowExpert Email Newsletter.
- HowExpert.com/books – HowExpert Books
- HowExpert.com/courses – HowExpert Courses
- HowExpert.com/clothing – HowExpert Clothing
- HowExpert.com/membership – HowExpert Membership Site
- HowExpert.com/affiliates – HowExpert Affiliate Program
- HowExpert.com/jobs – HowExpert Jobs
- HowExpert.com/writers – Write About Your #1 Passion/Knowledge/Expertise & Become a HowExpert Author.
- HowExpert.com/resources – Additional HowExpert Recommended Resources
- YouTube.com/HowExpert – Subscribe to HowExpert YouTube.
- Instagram.com/HowExpert – Follow HowExpert on Instagram.
- Facebook.com/HowExpert – Follow HowExpert on Facebook.
- TikTok.com/@HowExpert – Follow HowExpert on TikTok.

Made in the USA
Las Vegas, NV
07 October 2023

78726080R00059